It is only imperfection that complains of what is imperfect. The more perfect we are, the more gentle and quiet we become towards the defects of others.

- Françios Fénelon

The Silent Voice

PogoPublishing, Inc.
217 East Bolton Street, Suite B
Savannah, Georgia 31401
U.S.A.

Editorial Design
Amy Long
suprememajestyofever@gmail.com

Dust Jacket Design
Nancy Hyer
nanhyer@att.net

Website Design
Red Tusk Studios
www.redtusk.com

Limited Edition • May 2012
ISBN 978-1-4675-2712-5

Text and Photographs
Copyright © 2012

All rights reserved

Any part of this book may be reproduced with the
written consent of the publisher.

Printed and bound in the United States of America

Contents

Acknowledgements	VI
Author's Note	VIII
Introduction	IX
Profiles	7
Apologue	186
Do You Know?	190
Ask Yourself	191
A Suggested Solution	192
It's Up To Us	194
Appendices	197
About The Author	200

Acknowledgements

For the direction I have been given through her Inspiration, Love, and Support I am most thankful to my teacher and wife, Arlene.

I am deeply grateful to the following people, without whom this project may have never been completed: Myoshin Kelley; Joel Osteen; Arlene Meyer; Jan, Michelle, and Charlotte; Karen and Ed; Lukas Johnson; Jamie; Jez, Jennifer, Bill; Birgit and Robert; Steven and Julie; Lynn and Sarah Leah; Al and Dee; Henry and Nancy; Will and Gail; Al and Beanie; Brian; Brad and Sue Ann; Heather Dewar; Ward Parker; Amber; Sandra; Edna and Abigail; Barbara and Lenny; Bob; Ted and Nancy; Alice, Shannon, and Joshua; Oregon and Dottie; Art and Phyllis; Bill Weaver; John Miller; Amy; Quincy; Ryan; John; Karen and Evan, Melanie; Charles; Travis; Kesha; Brian Goble; Martha Ann; Spring; Ryann Hyer; Mary LaCalle; Mike Hasson; Steven Lopata and staff; Dick and Nancy; Jeff Markowsky. I am also grateful to the hundreds of anonymous people who have befriended me and shown me "the way" in each city that I visited; and especially to my friend, Joan, for her constant encouragement, expertise, emails, and love. A special thanks to my high school teacher and friend, Sabra Qua, who inspired me to believe that I was much more than I thought I was; and to my Aunt Kitty, who loved me before I was able to love myself.

You have all made many lives better through your presence and willingness to serve.

This book is affectionately
dedicated to those who were,
are,
and will be homeless...

and
to God,
whose grace
lovingly looks after them.

Author's Note

This book was conceived out of concern for the homeless in this country.

Its purpose is to raise awareness, especially among our elected public servants, to pass compassionate legislation which would help to resolve the condition of homelessness in America.

I am hopeful that this book will give a voice to this silent minority; would make them real rather than invisible; would effect a dialogue of our feelings with them; and would initiate positive changes within each of our hearts regarding this situation that affects us all at some level.

I have spoken with homeless people in every state and this book contains bits of what some of them shared with me about their lives. No attempt was made to verify the authenticity of the information received durring these discussions.

It is my hope that these pages will help to uncover a greater understanding of what it was like, what hapened, and what it's like now for some of America's homeless.

Introduction

September 1992 - Hurricane Andrew has just leveled South Florida. The streets of downtown Miami are rapidly filling with traumatized men, women, and children who have lost loved ones and homes. People have come from other parts of the country to find employment and help rebuild the area, now some of them are homeless too.

The Homestead Air Force Base near Miami has been evacuated by the military. Why isn't The Federal Emergency Management Agency (FEMA) using the vacated base as a shelter? Could not some of the barracks be refurbished? What about providing a small room for the homeless person who wants a new start in life or just needs a safe place to sleep? If inmates are entitled to food, shelter, clothing, warmth, televisions, medical care, and education, should not a homeless person who has committed no crime at least be entitled to a small, safe space of his or her own?

Nevertheless, these questions of mine go unanswered because I was committed to other projects at that time. Of course, like most other concerned citizens, I volunteered to help out whenever I could.

As the years went by, I kept asking myself many questions: Just who is it that is homeless? What is her name? What is his name? In what town was she raised? In what town is he trying to live now? Did she ever work? If so, what did she do? What happened? How does he feel? How did he fall into this world of broken hearts and shattered dreams? What, if anything, would that person, he or she, like to say to the rest of us?

September 2004 - I went on a four-week retreat and during the third week of silence a voice - a quiet, but firm Voice said, "Write a book about homelessness." A friend with whom I was sharing this vision knew that one of my hobbies was hopping around on my pogo stick. He said, in all seriousness, "Why don't you get a small camera and a recorder and pogo around the country interviewing homeless people?"

I thought that was the dumbest idea I'd heard in a long time and tried to dismiss it from my mind but found that I could not. Four months later I began planning to pogo through all fifty states and talk with homeless people along the way.

In 2005, I pogoed through all of the Eastern States (from Florida to Maine, and from South Carolina to Kentucky) visiting with the homeless in parks, on the streets, on the grounds of State Capitol buildings, next to City Halls, in the woods, in libraries, in the ghetto, and in well-to-do neighborhoods.

In 2006, I pogoed throughout the Midwest (from Texas to North Dakota, from Missouri to Colorado) and in the state of Hawaii. In 2007, I pogoed through the Western States (from Arizona to Alaska and from Utah to California) listening to stories and taking photographs when appropriate.

I loved hopping around the country on my pogo stick and most of the homeless people loved seeing me come. For them, I suppose, it was both humorous and amazing to see a 65-year-old man with a long white beard pogoing into their neighborhood. It was as though my pogoing was a bright light illuminating their dark world. This simple non-threatening act opened the door for them to receive my request for an interview; they trusted me and shared openly and honestly with language that was always from the heart.

September 1, 2010 - Here are Bobby, Susan, Peter, Shayla, and many more with whom I have become acquainted. Bobby is a former millionaire, Susan a paralegal, Peter a Phi Beta Kappa, and Shayla a pregnant teenager. Here is a child not much older than your own who lives like America's garbage, on the side streets in cardboard boxes or shivering beside a wall next to the convention center in Cleveland, Ohio.

Here are their faces. Here are their names. Some are smiling, some scowl at demons. What does the homeless person most desire? A small room with a bed? A safe space of their own where they can sleep and keep their meager belongings? Just a little room of their own, however small? Or maybe just a little respect and a kind word as we pass them on our way to the office?

Please take my hand and come with me as we travel through the pages of this book and look into the eyes and lives of some of these forgotten people. Consider the possibility that misunderstanding can be replaced by an empathetic recognition of someone else's nature or situation, thereby transforming feelings of suspicion, hatred, and fear into tolerance, peace, and love. I am hopeful that in "The Silent Voice" the cry of the homeless will be heard - not just by our eyes and ears but within our hearts.

Somewhere in America
2005

How did I get here?

What's going to happen to me?

Atlanta, Georgia
2005

Joseph

What it was like
Joseph was a happily married man. He had a nice home and wonderful children.

What happened
While reading the newspaper in his living room, he heard unusual sounds coming from the kitchen. He ran in to see his wife convulsing on the floor and his two year old daughter next to her, dead. The electric stove had shorted out and electrocuted them both. His wife died two weeks later in the hospital. After three years in a mental hospital, he was released and took up residence on the streets of Atlanta. His mother raised his other children.

What it's like now
Joseph is kind, gentle and thoughtful; he has been homeless for ten years. Initially he gave up on life, but today he has dedicated himself to helping others who are homeless, primarily homeless children.

I tried to turn off the stove but the power threw me against the wall.
- Joseph

Portland, Maine
2005

Cheryl

What it was like
Cheryl was in the T.V. and broadcasting business; she volunteered for the Democratic Headquarters and had a husband, son, and nice home.

What happened
She and her husband separated and soon thereafter she became disabled with a degenerative disease. Because she was unable to work any longer, she lost her home.

What it's like now
Homeless since 1999, she and her companion, Jim, live in an A-frame that Jim built in the "Hobo Forest," a shantytown where otherwise homeless people live near downtown Portland. She receives $10 each month in Food Stamps and $579 in Supplemental Security Income through a federal program that supports people with disabilities. Cheryl is the kind of person you would want as your next-door neighbor: strong, compassionate, helpful, open, kind, and with a heart of gold.

It really hurts when someone yells at me, 'Old lady get a job.' If they only knew. It's frustrating trying to work with agencies. They don't seem to know how to communicate with each other effectively and as a result we don't get the kind of help or understanding we need.
- Cheryl

Denver, Colorado
2006

Patrick

What it was like
Patrick was born and raised in Denver, and he worked as a landscaping contractor. He was earning over $2,000 each week.

What happened
While he was on his way to the bank with a deposit, two men attempted to rob him. Patrick defended himself and severely beat one of the attackers. He was arrested for assault and battery and sentenced to one year in jail.

What it's like now
Patrick was recently released and is working as a bouncer; he is able to sleep and shower occasionally at the houses of his friends. He is very friendly, peaceful, and philosophical, and spends most of his days reading and enjoying the grounds around the State Capitol building in Denver, Colorado.

This is just another page of my life.   - Patrick

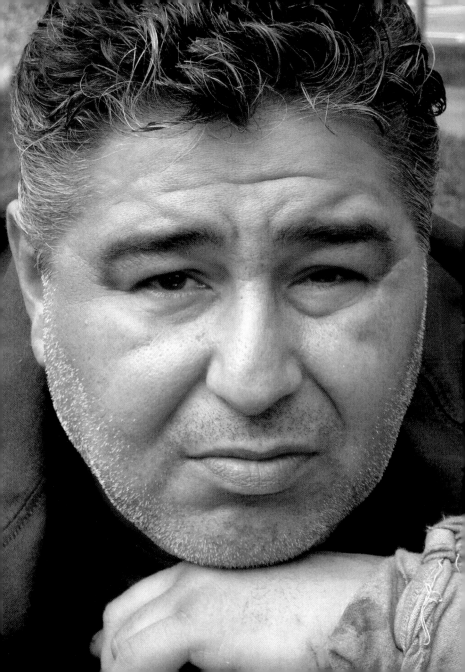

New York, New York
2005

Evita

What it was like
Evita was born in Jamaica, but she moved to New York, was married, divorced and had one son who has since died. She attended nursing school and cared for the sick and suffering for many years.

What happened
After her divorce, she moved to Florida. She decided to move back to New York after she was robbed. After arriving back in New York with little or no money, she found she could no longer afford the rent there.

What it's like now
Evita has a combined accent of British and Spanish and when she speaks it is more like a song than mere words. She sleeps on the streets and eats at soup kitchens. She has a wonderful personality and sparkling eyes. She is a delight to be with and if you look deeply enough you can see the rare beauty she once was. She admits that she is much more attractive with teeth, but the lack of them won't keep her from smiling.

God takes care of me every day. God bless our country.
  - Evita

Miami, Florida
2005

Obie

What it was like
Obie is 49 years old and was born into a Bahamian alcoholic household in Miami. He is intelligent, was a gifted athlete, and thought he was going to make it in society. Once, he was married, and had a home and children.

What happened
A steel cable broke at his jobsite and it backlashed, fracturing his skull and shoulder. Following extensive surgery and rehabilitation he was finally put on disability and, not having sufficient income, lost his home and family.

What it's like now
Having been homeless for 20 years, he has a number of medical problems and thinks he is just waiting to die. In the meantime, he feels a calling from God to be a champion of other homeless people and tries to help everyone on South Beach as much as possible.

There is nothing like your own family and home. If you have a family you are blessed. Don't lose them. I know both sides of having a family and not having them. Be grateful - you may be a paycheck or two away from homelessness. I'd love to have my own home where my grandchildren could come to visit and watch TV. I pray that you don't ever have to be here.   - Obie

Harrisburg, Pennsylvania
2005

Mary Ellen

What it was like

Mary Ellen was born in Scranton, Pennsylvania. She has been working since she was seventeen. She is married to Bill; they have two children.

What happened

After separating from Bill she became involved with another man who molested and kidnapped the daughter they had together. She then moved into a shelter.

What it's like now

Although she was working while living in the shelter, she was laid off and because her time was up she had to leave the shelter. She has been homeless for two weeks now, and she has reunited with her ex-husband Bill. Both of them are currently living in a tent in the woods.

I'm ready to cry. Homelessness is taking its toll on me. I have no I.D. so I cannot get a job. I get dirty looks from people. I've always worked. Anyone can fall from the top to the bottom and it can happen real fast, too. Please don't ever take life for granted because you never know when this could happen to you. My dream is to make Bill's favorite chicken recipe again and have a home once more.
- Mary Ellen

Las Vegas, New Mexico
2006

Charles

What it was like
Charles is 60 years old, was born in San Francisco and appears to be mentally challenged. He is unable to recall childhood events, but does remember that he graduated high school and worked in a department store.

What happened
He lost interest in working after being passed over for promotions numerous times by college graduates. He has been homeless for 35 years.

What it's like now
Yes, there really is a Las Vegas, New Mexico where he lives under bridges, on the desert, and in the woods where animals like to sleep next to him. His clothes and the blanket he uses as a bag are all torn up. He is filthy and the stench from him is awful but his soul is pure. His lips and fingers are charred from smoking cigarettes down to nothing. He speaks softly with a slow southern drawl, which is very engaging, and his eyes are bright as the color of the desert sky. He says little but is very polite, humble, and grateful for what little he has. I fought to hold back tears and release the knot in my stomach as I watched this poor man hobble slowly along the highway. He is so pathetic...so tired...and so worn out. Opening his blanket, he said...

You may have whatever you like.   - Charles

Worcester, Massachusetts
2005

Eileen

What it was like
Eileen was born in Worcester, Massachusetts; She was married, had three children, and a home.

What happened
Eileen and her husband separated and she became a single parent. Following the removal of a kidney, and with an ongoing arthritic back condition, she could no longer work and lost her home.

What it's like now
Eileen has been homeless for only four months, and she feels sad and disgusted that she is in this situation. Some people are cruel to her but most are kind and helpful and give her change at the street corner. She has tried to work but is unable. She has severe sunburn from standing on the corner. She has been denied disability income because she does not have a permanent address. She alternates between sleeping on the streets and staying at the homes of friends. Eileen is friendly, polite and humble.

It's hard to get out. I need help. I can't understand why we can't stay in abandoned buildings. My dream is to have a home again... and if I do I would let some homeless people stay with me. Today I understand.
— Eileen

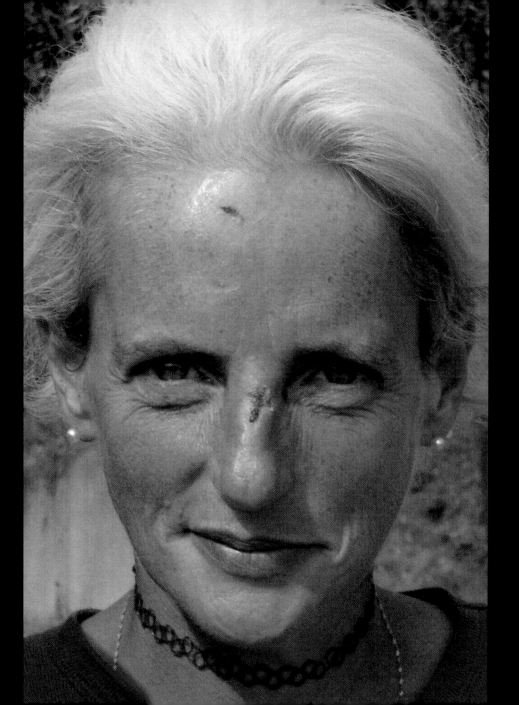

Key West, Florida
2005

Michael

What it was like
Michael was born in San Diego, California and has lived in Key West, Florida for the past one and a half years.

What happened
He became disabled and has a difficult time communicating.

What it's like now
He spends his days just watching people. He has been through three hurricanes this year and manages to survive them by staying close to a wall. He watched as the wind picked up a man and threw him over the street and into another wall. Michael's eyes are deeply penetrating. It's not so much that he can see through you but that he can see into you.

Observing people is my spiritual calling. It's what I do best.
- Michael

Charleston, West Virginia
2005

Susan

What it was like
Susan is a college graduate; she also attended graduate school and became a paralegal. She used to earn in excess of $53,000 a year.

What happened
She lost her mother, then her dog, and became depressed. She then moved to Charleston, where she was unable to earn more than $10 per hour, fell behind on her rent and then was evicted.

What it's like now
She has been homeless for six months; she volunteers at the local shelter and is currently sleeping on a shelf in an abandoned walk-in freezer. She has brilliant green eyes that turn blue naturally. She is happy, friendly, and helpful.

I didn't realize I could live on $10 an hour. Now I know I can live on $6.50 an hour. I used to feel that my furniture was so important. Please treat homeless people with respect. The police treat me with more respect than most people do.   - Susan

Baltimore, Maryland
2005

If a man has enough to live on, and yet when he sees his brother in need shuts up his heart against him, how can it be said that the divine Love dwells in him?
- John

Honolulu, Hawaii
2007

"J"

What it was like
"J" was born in Pittsburgh to parents who abused him. He studied Classical Guitar at Carnegie Mellon University as well as Business Administration at the University of Pittsburgh.

What happened
He was general manager of a restaurant but heavily involved with drugs. He moved to Hawaii with his girlfriend. Eventually they broke up, he became depressed, and could no longer function well enough to cover the cost of housing in Honolulu. He has been homeless for the past two years.

What it's like now
"J" no longer uses drugs and works sporadically as a messenger or in construction but is unable to come up with enough money for rent. Without a permanent address or phone he is unable to get a real job. He wishes he had never moved to Hawaii because it is so expensive, however, living on the streets has given him tools for survival and he feels good about his independence and freedom. He prefers to earn his own income, and thus does not panhandle.

I would love a place to keep my instruments, to play music professionally and have some cash flow again.   *- "J"*

Hartford, Connecticut
2005

Bob

What it was like

Bob is a college graduate, Korean War Veteran, and worked for 39 years as a security advisor. He has traveled to 19 countries on business.

What happened

Bob's wife died and shortly thereafter several other members of his family died in rapid succession. Bob became deeply depressed and went over the edge. He was institutionalized and heavily sedated. After his savings ran out and the insurance payments stopped, an attorney had him sign papers leaving everything to the hospital to cover expenses. He was still sedated when he was released from the hospital, and thought they were taking him home but instead the ambulance took him to the shelter where he has been for one and a half years.

What it's like now

Bob lives on his Social Security check, makes monthly payments of $78 to the hospital, and still owes thousands. He hates the shelter and the stench in the bathroom, which results from people having to go to the toilet but instead going in a basket because the lines are too long in the morning.

Until now I always wore suits. I never owned dungarees. Rob and I are hoping to pool our money together in August and find an inexpensive apartment together.   *- Bob*

Seattle, Washington
2007

Shayla

What it was like

Shayla had six brothers and one sister. They all lived with their mother, who was on welfare. They lived in shelters, cars, apartments, the houses of friends, and cheap hotels.

What happened

Because they were so poor, her mother asked her to leave when she was twelve years old. She has never gone back.

What it's like now

Shayla is now 19 years old. She has been living on the streets for the past seven years in Seattle. She has done some work in carnivals and in the food service industry. She is currently eight months pregnant and because she was unable to stay in a shelter, a private group of citizens called "Open Adoption" is currently providing her with a hotel room until the baby is born. She has met the adoptive parents to be and they all like each other. Upon birth she will give up her baby but will have visitation privileges. Shayla is quiet, humble, peaceful, and has a beautiful spirit. She is loveable, mature, and wise.

I miss my brothers and sister. My dream is to own a carnival and be married. Live your life and don't worry about things that don't matter. Live from your heart and not from your pocketbook.   - Shayla

Providence, Rhode Island
2005

Michael

What it was like
Known affectionately as "Cowboy" to all his friends, Michael served in Vietnam in the rice paddies but was later shot in San Antonio, Texas. He had a home and two cars in the driveway.

What happened
His Supplemental Security Income was cut off and he then became homeless. What little money he had left was stolen while he was hitchhiking. After consuming a half-gallon of vodka, he went into a coma for 36 days and was unable to speak or walk.

What it's like now
He has since recovered and has also lost a substantial amount of weight. Michael has been "riding the rails" for years and has faithfully attended the National Hobo Convention held annually in Britt, Iowa. He writes poetry and sings. Recently married, he now lives in a tent with his wife, Geneva. It's obvious he's in love with her and his eyes sparkle like those of an innocent child.

I hate living like this. The police constantly harass us and shelters won't let husbands and wives stay together. I'd like to return to Albuquerque and settle down into a nice home. We trust in God to take care of us.
- Michael

Philadelphia, Pennsylvania
2005

Start learning to love God by loving those whom you cannot love. The more you remember others with kindness and generosity, the more you forget yourself and when you forget yourself completely, you find God.

- Meher Baba

Austin, Texas
2006

A.J.

What it was like

A.J. was born in Providence, Rhode Island. He grew up in a normal, happy family. He spent 2 years in the military, then was employed for the last 20 years as a cabinetmaker. He has never married but has a 20-year-old daughter whom he hasn't seen for eight years. He is 45 years old.

What happened

A chronic alcoholic, he drank himself out of his career. He has been homeless for the past three years and is currently living on the streets in Austin, Texas.

What it's like now

He says living on the streets "sucks" and he always has to watch his back. He constantly worries about food, where to sleep, gangs, and the police. Although he panhandles on corners with his sign and receives about $30 a day, he prefers to eat from dumpsters. He wants to stop drinking but has not been able to. He says that most people are nice to him. He does have a rather engaging personality, and he is intelligent, helpful, sincere, and attentive.

I'd like to have my own place where I can feel safe and start all over again.
- A.J.

Columbia, South Carolina
2005

Sylvia

What it was like
Sylvia was born in Munich, Germany; she majored in Chemistry in college and worked as a lab technician.

What happened
She was married to a man who abused drugs and kept inviting his drug-abusing friends to move in. She got hooked and used heroin for 17 years. She is now divorced and on the streets, and sleeps on the ground behind a church.

What it's like now
At age 55 she is filled with cancer. Free from heroin, she now drinks to kill the pain. She bathes in the river. She spends her days at the temporary labor pool waiting for work and reading. Soup lines for women are only at noon and if she gets a job she cannot eat lunch. She prostitutes herself for food. She hates her situation and is frustrated with the "system." People "treat her like dirt".

I would like to ask everyone to read Ecclesiastes Chapter 3 and First Corinthians Chapter 13.*
- Sylvia

* *Please see Appendices I and II*

Cleveland, Ohio
2005

Mike

What it was like
Mike was born in Cleveland, Ohio; he has spent years in Texas and worked in the landscaping business.

What happened
He became homeless six years ago when he was unable to put together enough work and money.

What it's like now
An excellent communicator, he feels that many homeless people have more sense than "normal" people. He feels that being homeless is exciting, interesting, tragic, and funny but he is now getting tired of it.

I miss not being able to take a shower when I want to or watch TV when I'd like to. Someday we all die and someday everything could be taken from us. I know a man who was a millionaire who now lives on the streets. A lot of us feel that agencies are trying to regulate our lives when all we want is some help, some guidance and to be listened to and not treated like little children. We used to be "normal" people. We are not aliens. Please be sincere, down to earth and respectful.
- Mike

Philadelphia, Pennsylvania
2005

Mary

What it was like
Mary was married and lived in an apartment in Philadelphia.

What happened
Mary's husband died and she continued doing housework for income but she could not produce enough money by herself so her landlord evicted her.

What it's like now
Mary is in her mid-60's and has been living on the streets, wherever she can find a spot, for two years. She is very thin, and she has to beg for food or enough money to eat. She is sincere, honest, polite, humble and desperate. She is timid, scared, and does not know how to live like this. She asked that her photograph not be taken.

Mary is a beautiful woman and her story is heartbreaking. I felt as though I was standing in the presence of God when I listened to her. I felt goose bumps and continued crying for a block after I left her. Princess Diana would have held her close.   - Editor

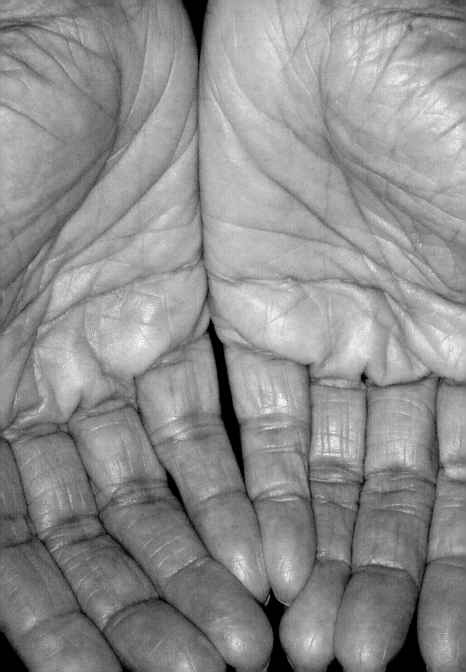

Sitka, Alaska
2007

The best way to find yourself is to lose yourself in the service of others.

- Ghandi

Boston, Massachusetts
2005

Ronnie

What it was like
Ronnie's family came to the United States from New Guinea. His mother was mentally ill and never knew him. His father "didn't give a s---." His grandfather, who had raised seven other children in a small truck, also brought him up.

What happened
Ronnie left home at an early age to live on the streets. He was a "mean motherf-----," broke his hands many times and lived in dangerous places.

What it's like now
Ronnie has been homeless for over 30 years, he has mended his ways, but is an admitted alcoholic. He's been through a "lot of s---." He cleans up the area where he stays and collects bottles and cans for income. He eats from dumpsters and admits he is confused. He has no dreams about the future other than getting ready for the winter (which he was doing in July). He has seen several friends freeze to death because they refused to get up and keep moving. He feeds the birds and dogs in the area and he began to cry as he expressed sadness about his mother dying and the fact that he did not know of her death for four months.

I have mellowed a lot. God bless you. - Ronnie

Seattle, Washington
2007

Jason

What it was like
Jason grew up with his parents in a suburb of Sacramento, and feels that his parents took good care of him.

What happened
He was in college but ran out of money for tuition. He then moved in with a "friend" who cheated him out of what little money he had left.

What it's like now
Jason is 23 and has been on the streets for three years. He harbors no resentment toward his "friend" and has come to discover that living on the streets is a real education in itself. He loves having the freedom to do what he wants to do and feels that living on the streets is better than having things given to him. He is able to lie on broken glass and is learning how to eat it. He hopes to establish himself in Europe by doing whatever makes him happy. He is currently looking for a teacher who will show him the next creative thing he is destined to learn. Jason is a beautiful human being and very wise for his age.

The universe is big and beautiful so be more aware of the world around you by taking the time to look beyond yourself. Consider others and the world as a whole.   - *Jason*

Miami, Florida
2005

Patty

What it was like

Patty lived on Miami Beach and had been working at a bagel shop for one year. She has been employed all of her life until now. She had an apartment and walked her dog each morning before reporting for work at 5 A.M.

What happened

Patty became ill and was replaced at the shop. She was evicted before she could overcome her illness and find other employment.

What it's like now

Patty has been homeless for four months. Her clothes have been stolen and she is mistreated by "normal" people who tell her to get a job. She has tried desperately to find work. She is willing to do anything. She pan handles and may get $4 per day. She does not drink or smoke and has a "heart of gold" according to those who know her. She sleeps in the park and eats food from the church.

It is so hard being homeless. I am 50 years old and have never been in trouble. I just want to get off the streets and have a job and a home again.
- Patty

Anchorage, Alaska
2007

Bobby

What it was like
Bobby was born in Howell, Iowa. He grew up with a mom, dad, and six siblings. His father was a minister for 45 years. Bobby was married and had one daughter.

What happened
Bobby was once a millionaire. He made his money in the meat slaughter and packing business following his years in the rice paddies of Vietnam where his friends were killed or maimed, or committed suicide upon their return. Following his divorce (in which his ex-wife was awarded all of his money), he retreated to Nome, Alaska where he became disabled and discouraged with life and lost the remainder of his meager estate. He "just gave up."

What it's like now
Bobby is now 58 years old and was beaten up by three teenagers last night. He holds a sign on a corner in Anchorage in the rain to gather enough coins to eat. He sleeps in a tent in the woods with fifteen other homeless men. He is friendly and helpful, and he maintains a sense of humor and says that laughter is the best medicine.

Lord, please help us. We can't do this alone. My dream is to have a nice wife and home again. — *Bobby*

Lake Tahoe, California
2007

A word, a smile, and the stranger at your elbow may become an interesting friend. All through life we deny ourselves stimulating fellowship because we are too proud or too afraid to unbend.

- D.C. Peattie

Pittsburgh, Pennsylvania
2008

Enola

What it was like
Enola was born in Pittsburgh; she lived with her family and graduated from high school.

What happened
After working at several jobs, she decided to move to California and discovered she loved traveling.

What it's like now
At 23 years old, she is a wanderlust at heart. She moves from place to place on the train riding in box cars, eating from dumpsters. She sleeps under bridges, in trees, parks, churches, or at houses of friends; she refuses to stay in shelters. She will occasionally pose nude for photographers and play music on her saw to earn a little income. She considers herself an anarchist and corresponds with political prisoners. She is a vegetarian and uses no drugs, alcohol, tobacco, or caffeine. She is adept in the art of self-defense and is rarely fearful. She loves her life and is courageous, cautious, intelligent, and has a warm, engaging personality. She plans to travel internationally and learn several foreign languages.

I am not homeless, I am 'home-free.' Please have respect for all other living things and realize it's not very hard to live without things that people think are necessities.   - Enola

Portland, Maine
2006

Jim

What it was like
When he was growing up in a foster home, Jim was hostile, angry, and discontented; he has had numerous run-ins with the law.

What happened
Jim met Cheryl and her loving, yet firm Spirit has changed Jim into a loyal and protective man who is always ready to help his friends. He is intelligent and is his own man. After being Injured, he was unable to work and thus lost their apartment in Portland, Maine.

What it's like now
Jim collects anything recyclable and had, at the time we met, over $200 in cans and bottles. He and Cheryl live in the woods in an A-frame, which he built in seven days with his bare hands, a bow saw, and limbs from surrounding trees. He is the last Gate Keeper of "The Hobo Forest" in Portland, Maine.

This land has been here for the homeless for over 100 years and is now being taken over by a hospital who wants us out by Monday.
- Jim

Trenton, New Jersey
2005

Life ain't quite what I thought it'd be, but, then, death will probably surprise me, too.

- Edna Meyer

Brattleboro, Vermont
2005

Kate

What it was like
Kate came from a happy, normal home in Philadelphia where her parents have continued to live since Kate was born. She has attended four years of art school.

What happened
Kate met Jesson, they married and decided to live an alternative lifestyle.

What it's like now
Kate is happily married, works as an artist's model, and is in the food service business. She earns a good income and paints but has decided not to spend her money on an apartment or car. She loves living close to and experiencing nature. She and Jesson will sleep anywhere and are currently living in a tent in the woods.

I feel very close to community living this way. I want to always be a woman of integrity and be very open and fulfilled as an artist.
- Kate

Raleigh, North Carolina
2005

Wilber

What it was like
Wilber was unmarried, worked as a supervisor in a nursing home, had a nice home and two cars.

What happened
When his hours were cut back, he began getting behind on car payments, rent, insurance, and credit cards; he finally lost it all.

What it's like now
Wilber is a beautiful man with a wonderful heart. He has been on the streets for three years. He sleeps on the ground and has often been fined $180 for sleeping in public, so he now sleeps with one eye open, watching for the police. He waits in soup lines of 300 to 400 for his meals and has developed patience, tolerance, and integrity. He works regularly for the labor pool but cannot get a good job because he now has bad credit and a criminal record as a result of being homeless.

I feel good about life. I'm just hoping for a breakthrough. Get into a church where the Lord can work in your heart.   - Wilber

Savannah, Georgia
2007

Kathy

What it was like

Kathy was born in Jacksonville, Florida in 1958. Her parents divorced when she was three. Her mother then married a man who was verbally, emotionally, and sexually abusive to Kathy. She quit school in the eleventh grade to become a wife, mother and have a good family.

What happened

Her husband abused her. Within three years they divorced. She married a second time to a man who was kind but cheated on her. Following that divorce her ex-husband sold the house, took their 3 1/2-year-old daughter and disappeared. It has been 24 years since she last saw her daughter and "every day has been hard since."

What it's like now

Kathy has been homeless for four years now; she was evicted from the trailer park she was living in because she got into a relationship with a black man in a white trailer park. She has been living in her van in Savannah ever since.

The only thing that holds me together is God. When things are hard, good comes out of it. There is a reason for everything. It's God's plan. Somehow He has always provided for us.   -Kathy

Richmond, Virginia
2005

Ronald

What it was like
Ronald comes from an impoverished broken home. He always disliked school but enjoyed learning, and he served in the military. He was married with two children, drove a tractor trailer and had a home.

What happened
Although he had been married for 12 years, his income was going toward his drug use and his wife divorced him. Drugs took him down further until he lost everything.

What it's like now
Ronald is deeply philosophical, and he is a poet at heart. He works regularly two days a week and would like a full-time job but using grass keeps him from passing drug tests. He has been living on the streets for ten years. He visits with his grown daughter weekly at her dance school lesson. He is respectful and has a warm and beautiful Spirit.

We can know a lesson but it is not learned until it is applied productively. Live your own life but be willing to accept the consequences.   *- Ronald*

North Conway, New Hampshire
2005

White Feather

What it was like
White Feather was born in New Hampshire, where both of her parents were killed in an auto accident when she was nine. She was then adopted, and grew up with relatives on an Indian Reservation in Wyoming.

What happened
She joined the Army and while serving she was in a helicopter crash and both of her knees were broken.

What it's like now
She is retired from the military and receives just about enough compensation so that she doesn't have to work. Rather than having an apartment, she prefers sleeping on a cot or on the ground in her tent and essentially lives out of her van which houses all of her belongings including her cat. When we met, two friends had just given her a tepee.

I love to go to Pow Wows and I visit as many as I can. I do needlepoint, beadwork and make shawls. I even sell some for a little extra income. I'm O.K. as long as I don't have repair bills on my van.
- White Feather

Atlanta, Georgia
2005

Do not close your eyes before suffering. Find ways to be with those who are suffering by all means, including personal contact and visits. By such means, awaken yourself and others to the reality of suffering in the world.

- Gautama Buddha

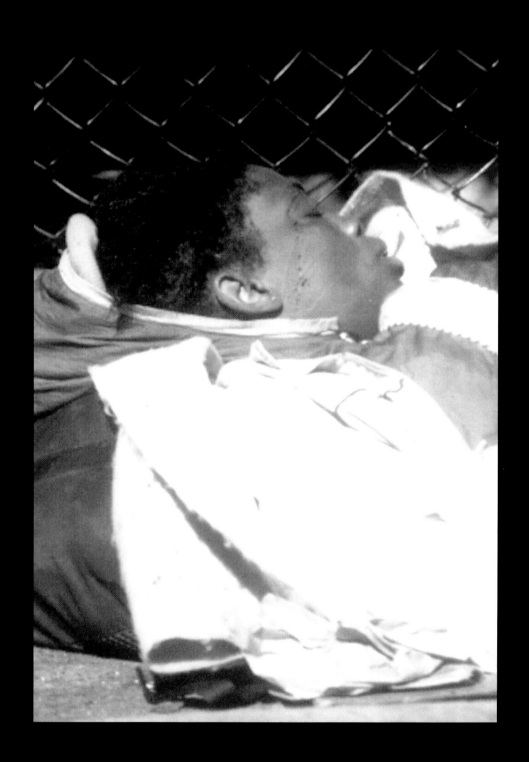

Arlington, Virginia
2005

Santiago

What it was like
Santiago was born in El Salvador, and has been living in this country with friends.

What happened
Because he was unable to support his share of the rent, he was asked to move out.

What it's like now
Having been homeless for two years now, Santiago was waiting with 20 other friends at a labor pool. When I met him he was able to find construction work only once or twice a week and has been unable to find affordable housing. He is friendly and willing to work full time.

If I had a home I would bring a homeless person to live with me. We just need affordable housing to help us build up our self esteem again. — *Santiago*

Hickory, North Carolina
2005

Tom

What it was like

Tom was born into a family of ten "mountain people" in West Virginia. Tom's father was killed by a train, his brother killed three men and one of his sisters is beaten regularly by her husband. When Tom was nine, his mother ran off with a man, leaving Tom to be raised by an older brother.

What happened

At the age of fifteen, Tom left home and was reported as "missing" for seven years.

What it's like now

Tom has been homeless for eighteen years. He makes a little money as a landscaper and he lives in the woods. Unable to settle down, he is restless and just travels back and forth across the United States year after year. His life has been an "adventure." He has been chased by a bear, has a good sense of humor, and likes to tell funny, often tragic, stories about his family and his life.

I do get lonely sometimes but I wouldn't have it any other way. Live your life like you mean it. If you are a female, stay off the streets.
- Tom

Half Moon, New York
2005

Katie

What it was like
Katie was from a "proper" home, involved in church and civic activities, and has a grandfather who was a senator. She was an honor student in high school and was accepted to Yale.

What happened
After attending college for one year she left to take care of her mother who was ill. Katie and her mother (who has been divorced and remarried three times) were unable to get along, so Katie was asked to leave.

What it's like now
Katie smokes cigarettes but does not use alcohol or drugs. She has been homeless off and on for about six years. She has been married and divorced and has a daughter who lives with her mother's sister. Katie works regularly and makes monthly payments on her college loan but is unable to accumulate enough to have her own place. She feels alone and stressed out but grateful that she has a roof over her head at the shelter.

My dream is to have a home and get my daughter back. Anyone can become homeless. It could happen to anyone.   *- Katie*

Washington, D. C.
2005

John

What it was like
John was born in Bingham, New York. He is a graduate of Syracuse University and has a master's degree in Library Science.

What happened
When he was unable to find a job that matched his education, he eventually went through his savings of $50,000. Discouraged, he ended up on the streets.

What it's like now
Having been homeless for seven years, he sleeps at bus stops and eats at soup kitchens. John is so nice. He is like a big teddy bear. He is gentle, humble, and thoughtful and has big, beautiful, sparkling blue eyes.

I feel the homeless situation will keep getting worse before it gets better. Housing is so expensive today.   - John

Montpelier, Vermont
2005

Mary Ellen

What it was like
Mary Ellen has been Sales Director for a hotel chain and has owned her own restaurant and several rental homes.

What happened
After she was exhausted and overworked, she drove herself to stay awake and regularly work for 36 hours straight while indulging in huge amounts of caffeine. Her behavior became so erratic from sleeplessness and caffeine she was sent to a mental rehabilitation center. She was misdiagnosed and prescribed a drug for mental illness. This caused considerable injury to her central nervous system, thus rendering her incapable of generating an income sufficient to cover her mortgages and other expenses.

What it's like now
To cover expenses and debts, she sold everything and then lived on her remaining savings until it ran out. Living on disability income and sleeping at a "Drop Inn," she is currently trying to sue the doctor and hospital that misdiagnosed her.

I used to be so happy, energetic and enthusiastic. It's difficult not being a smiling, vibrant person anymore. I am trying to be as positive as I can.
- Mary Ellen

Philadelphia, Pennsylvania
2005

Let us not be satisfied with just giving money. Money is not enough, money can be got, but they need your hearts to love them. So, spread your love wherever you go.

- Mother Teresa

Key West, Florida
2005

Ed

What it was like
Ed grew up in California. He was married and worked as an Optometrist. He is 53 years old.

What happened
His wife died and shortly thereafter Ed suffered a stroke, which paralyzed his left arm and legs so he could no longer practice his profession. He is confined to a wheelchair and suffers from gout. Although he is on disability income, it is not enough to cover his expenses.

What it's like now
Ed has been homeless for the past six years, and is known as "Speedy" by his friends. He eats at the soup kitchen and resides on the streets in Key West, Florida. He would like to go back to California to visit with his relatives sometime.

Don't be homeless. Go to church. - Ed

Dover, Delaware
2005

Mary

What it was like
Mary was born in Newark, New Jersey, has been deaf since birth, was married, and lived in a small home.

What happened
She and her husband divorced, and a "friend" of hers drove her down to Delaware, stole her two disability checks, and dropped her off at a shelter.

What it's like now
Although she worked at a fast food restaurant making salads, she was unable to accumulate enough money to get an apartment before her time ran out at the shelter. She then moved in with another deaf person who, unfortunately, was a drug addict and got Mary hooked. Now she is homeless, and is scheduled to enter a rehab soon. Mary is polite, shy, naive, and vulnerable.

Let go and let God. - Mary

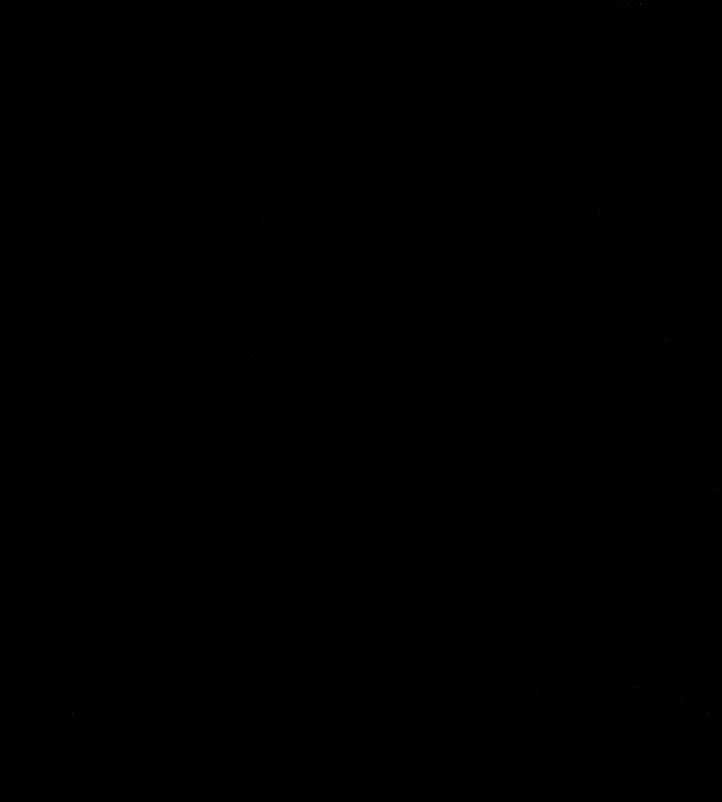

Montpelier, Vermont
2005

Peter

What it was like

Peter was born into an artistic family in St. Albans, Vermont; he was a Phi Beta Kappa and has a Masters Degree in Physics with a specialty in Acoustics. He was married and has one daughter. He was a piano tuner, an electronics repair person, and a music therapist for many years. Peter has participated in alternative energy projects and is fluent in German.

What happened

Years of heavy chronic drinking have taken their toll.

What it's like now

Peter is now 61; he no longer drinks and has been sober for several years. He still plays music and builds instruments. He is extremely intelligent and shares extensively about electronics, but not much about his feelings although he did begin to cry when he remembered his mother's tragic death. He is very friendly, kind, polite, and humble.

I have a car but it's not registered so I can't drive but I do sleep in it occasionally.
- Peter

Hinesville, Georgia
2009

Patricia and Ba-Shawn

What it was like
Patricia was married and had one son, Ba-Shawn, whose name is made up of syllables from relatives. Her life was fairly happy and her family enjoyed many activities together.

What happened
Her husband began working out of town and, over time, began coming home less frequently on weekends until he decided not to return at all. Because Patricia was unable to pay rent and living expenses, her landlord evicted her.

What it's like now
After being evicted in the winter of 2008, Patricia and her son stayed with a friend for two months, with an aunt for another week, and finally in a cheap motel for two weeks. A member of her church told her about an "Interfaith Hospitality" shelter where they stayed for another thirty days. She was then told about "The Next Step" program, which has provided them with a house. Patricia, who is a senior cook at Meals on Wheels, pays her own rent, "The Next Step" pays utilities, and ten percent of her income is put into a savings plan so that, in two years, she can own her own home.

I used to help homeless people so I never, in a million, years thought it would ever happen to me. Becoming homeless is devastating. If it weren't for the kindness of others we wouldn't be where we are today. Hang in there and have faith in God.   *- Patricia*

Apologue

Two years ago a friend of mine by the name of Walter was out west and picked up a homeless man by the side of the road near a town called Trinidad, Colorado. He had a limp, swollen stomach and was filthy. His stench was such that Walter had to keep the windows open as they drove along.

His name was Charles and he was heading to Santa Fe, New Mexico. He didn't say much but when he did, he was very pleasant and had beautiful blue eyes that matched the desert sky.

As they approached Las Vegas, New Mexico, Charles said he needed to get out and stretch his legs. He walked a little then sat on a curb. Walter brought him a hamburger, fries, a coke and coffee. Charles told Walter that if he wanted to go into town for an hour or so he would then be ready to travel on but if Walter needed to leave now it would be O.K. and he would get another ride.

Anxious to get on with his business in Santa Fe, Walter opted to leave but before he left, Charles told Walter he could have anything he wanted from his bag.

Charles' bag was a blanket, torn and filthy, and Walter assumed everything inside was, too. Walter told the man thank you, but no, he didn't need anything and took his leave.

Last year Walter had some business in Phoenix and quite by accident ran into an old friend from college whom he hadn't seen for thirty years. They agreed to meet for dinner and here is what his fraternity brother, David, told Walter:

"Two years ago I was in terrible shape. My business was failing, I was near bankruptcy and my home was about to be foreclosed. On top of that my wife of twenty-five years was threatening to leave me.

"During this time I had started becoming a little more religious and was praying constantly for God to help me but nothing seemed to happen.

"Desperate to make a sale, I went to Denver but was rejected by the purchasing agent. Extremely disappointed, I was actually considering suicide.

"On my return home I was exhausted and pulled off Interstate 25 in a little town called Las Vegas, New Mexico and went into a restaurant to get a cup of coffee. I had noticed a scraggly old man on the curb and ignored him as I went in but while in the restaurant I thought maybe that poor guy could use a cup of coffee.

"I handed it to him and he was, indeed, grateful and asked where I was going. 'Santa Fe,' I replied. He said that was where he was going and could I please give him a ride?

"My mind was reeling. Coffee…yes. Ride…no way! He looked terrible and smelled worse. I was thinking 'no' when much to my surprise, out of my mouth came the word, 'sure'.

"He told me his name was Charles and he was a nice enough fellow but was so smelly that I had to keep the windows open for fear that I might regurgitate. He drank coffee and smoked incessantly but said very little.

"When we arrived in Santa Fe I asked where he would like to go. He pointed towards a park down the street. Just as he was about to leave he opened his filthy blanket and said I could have anything I wanted. I could see that everything looked and smelled just like he did. But not wanting to disappoint him, I reached over and picked up a large stone with some metal twisted around it and said, 'Thank you'. I then shook his hand as he said, 'God blessed you,' not, ' God bless you,' as most people say, but almost prophetically, 'God blessed you.'

"My wife was pretty upset that I didn't make the sale in Denver but when I emptied my pockets she looked at the stone and said, 'what's this?'

"I told her the story about the homeless man and how he offered me whatever I wanted. She picked up the strange looking rock he had given me and, turning it over in her hands said, 'We need to get this appraised'.

"An appraisal revealed that the 'rock' was actually a large and precious gemstone.

"As a result of my interaction with this stranger, I felt as though my life has been restored. I opened my door for him and he opened my heart for me. I have often heard that it is better to give than to receive; but sometimes, I think, receiving is also an act of graciousness because, if we refuse, it robs the giver of an opportunity to be blessed."

Could it be that David's prayers were actually answered by the hand of God through the disguise of a homeless person and his willingness to be of service to him? I may never know, but this I do know – Walter's story has shown me a level of compassion that I have, heretofore, completely overlooked in my own life.

I've recently thought about the parallel between that poor, homeless man and an apparently worthless rock, and realize that most people pass by both – not recognizing the potential beauty that lies just beneath the surface.

Note: As a result of his good fortune David was able to purchase an abandoned warehouse which he renovated into 120 small 8' x 8' rooms and several larger ones for families so that every homeless person could have a safe place to call their own. They each have their own key, a bed, a sink, closet and small desk. They share bathrooms, phones, and a community dining room. Because they have a permanent address and phone most are able to find employment, which, heretofore, they could not.

Inspired by David's compassion, residents and businesses have united to bring about the restoration of other properties, rehabilitation for individuals, and have developed a park the residents can call their own.

His city no longer has homeless men, women, children, or families living on the streets.

Do You Know...

23% are mentally ill?

14% are single women?

3% are unaccompanied minors?

Only 30% use alcohol or drugs?

33% of homeless people are veterans?

17% actually have full or part time jobs?

40% of homeless are families with children?

Some homeless people actually freeze to death?

Over 12 million adults have been homeless at some point?

10% are so chronic that they are unable to be rehabilitated?

It costs much less to house a homeless person than an inmate?

Lack of affordable housing is a primary cause of homelessness?

These figures are approximate and statistics vary due to the transient nature of the homeless.

Ask Yourself...

Do I have an emergency or prudent reserve fund securely in place so that if I lose my job or get sick or injured I will still be able to make my rent or mortgage payments and cover my expenses for the next four to six months?

Am I courting financial disaster by spending more than I earn?

What would happen to me if my identity were stolen?

Do I have friends or relatives I could stay with if necessary?

At today's minimum wage, would I be willing to work 83 hours per week just to afford low cost housing?

Do I treat people today the way I would like to be treated tomorrow?

A Suggested Solution

Before we look at the solution to homelessness we need to understand what the problem is.

The problem is apathy. Apathy in me and apathy in you. Apathy in the hearts and minds of America.

Tonight there may be over five-hundred thousand children without homes and an equal number of families housed in shelters that may not be able to provide proper medical, rehabilitative, and/or counseling services.

Most homeless people can overcome their situation if they are given the opportunity. Although knowing why a person became homeless is relevant, it is our attitude, yours and mine, toward these fellow human beings that is really important.

A stable environment is the beginning of the solution. Our tax dollars provide America's inmates with food, shelter, clothing, warmth, medical care, and education. Should not a homeless person at least be entitled to a safe space of his or her own? Perhaps we can provide these same essentials for much less.

The magnitude of the homeless situation is such that it is beyond the aid of charitable groups alone. This is a national challenge that needs to be addressed through the combined services of government, the business community, and the active involvement of private citizens.

Homelessness has been around for centuries. Is there no solution? I think there is a solution. And it is really quite simple.

A. Government buildings, which have already been paid for by our tax dollars, that are currently vacant could be restored to house the homeless, and vacated military bases could also be utilized. I suggest that these properties be donated by the government and then operated by those in the private sector who are experienced in managing such facilities.

B. Businesses could financially contribute to the restoration and operational expenses of these facilities.

C. Charities and religious/spiritual groups could provide professional personnel and volunteers to help with the restoration of these buildings and rehabilitation of the homeless. The homeless themselves have a vested interest in this work, which can be exhibited through participation at all levels of the overall restoration and continued functioning of these facilities.

It is up to us...

"It's possible to overcome apathy with hope."
- Dr. Jane Goodall

    Social change begins with you and me. It begins with the belief that something could be better. And then it takes the willingness to commit ourselves to that change by taking the action necessary to bring about the desired results.

    If you would like to be a part of the solution, please take a moment and go to your phone or computer right now and contact your local congressperson. Ask him or her about establishing or supporting legislation that will bring about this change. Perhaps you may wish to send him or her a copy of this book; if so, please order from:

www.PogoPublishing.org

To learn more about homelessness, please visit

www.nationalhomelessness.org

If you would like to order additional copies of this book for your school, library, legislators, or friends, please visit:

www.PogoPublishing.org

or visit your local bookstore.

Feeling that it would be unethical to benefit from the misfortunes of others, the author has declined any compensation, asking that 100% of the net income from the distribution or sales of this book be dedicated to the solution of homelessness in America.

Appendix I

Ecclesiastes Chapter 3

For everything there is a season, and a time for every matter under heaven:
A time to be born, and a time to die;
A time to plant, and a time to pluck up what is planted;
A time to kill, and a time to heal;
A time to break down, and a time to build up;
A time to weep, and a time to laugh;
A time to mourn, and a time to dance;
A time to throw away stones, and a time to gather stones together;
A time to embrace, and a time to refrain from embracing;
A time to seek, and a time to lose;
A time to keep, and a time to throw away;
A time to tear, and a time to sew;
A time to keep silence, and a time to speak;
A time to love, and a time to hate;
A time for war, and a time for peace.
What gain have the workers for their toil? I have seen the business that God has given to everyone to be busy with. He has made everything suitable for its time; moreover he has put a sense of past and future into their minds, yet they cannot find out what God has done from the beginning to the end. I know that there is nothing better for them than to be happy and enjoy themselves as long as they live; moreover, it is God's gift that all should eat and drink and take pleasure in all their toil. I know that whatever God does endures forever; nothing can be added to it, nor anything taken from it; God has done this, so that all shall stand in awe before Him. That which is, already has been; that which is to be, already is; and God seeks out what has gone by.
Moreover I saw under the sun that in the place of justice, wickedness was there, and in the place of righteousness, wickedness was there as well. I said in my heart, God will judge the righteous and the wicked, for he has appointed a time for every matter, and for every work. I said in my heart with regard to human beings that God is testing them to show that they are but animals. For the fate of humans and the fate of animals is the same; as one dies, so dies the other. They all have

the same breath, and humans have no advantage over the animals; for all is vanity. All go to one place; all are from the dust, and all turn to dust again. Who knows whether the human spirit goes upward and the spirit of animals goes downward to the earth? So I saw that there is nothing better than that all should enjoy their work, for that is their lot; who can bring them to see what will be after them?

New Revised Standard Version.

Appendix II

First Corinthians Chapter 13

If I speak in the tongues of mortals and of angels, but do not have love, I am a noisy gong or a clanging cymbal. And if I have prophetic powers, and understand all mysteries and all knowledge, and if I have all faith, so as to remove mountains, but do not have love, I am nothing. If I give away all my possessions, and if I hand over my body so that I may boast, but do not have love, I gain nothing.

Love is patient; love is kind; love is not envious or boastful or arrogant or rude. It does not insist on its own way; it is not irritable or resentful; it does not rejoice in wrongdoing, but rejoices in the truth. It bears all things, believes all things, hopes all things, endures all things.

Love never ends. But as for prophecies, they will come to an end; as for tongues, they will cease; as for knowledge, it will come to an end. For we know only in part, and we prophesy only in part; but when the complete comes, the partial will come to an end. When I was a child, I spoke like a child, I thought like a child, I reasoned like a child; when I became an adult, I put an end to childish ways. For now we see in a mirror, dimly, but then we will see face to face. Now I know only in part; then I will know fully, even as I have been fully known. And now faith, hope, and love abide, these three; and the greatest of these is love.

New Revised Standard Version.

The Author

Christopher believes that his purpose is simply to carry this message from the homeless to you, the reader of this book.

Once homeless himself, he found a new life through a recovery program. He then went on to become a co-founder of a retreat center in Florida.

Today he carries a message of hope to the residents in a nearby correctional facility and lives with his lovely wife, two cats, and their dog in Savannah, Georgia.

He enjoys playing ping-pong with his wife, attending classical concerts, the ballet, and bicycling.

He gave his pogo stick to his brother on his 65th birthday.

"The test of our progress is not whether we add more to the abundance of those who have much; it is whether we provide enough for those who have too little." F.D.R.